"Leave it to the sensationally gifted Nikki Grimes to weld her devotions into one glorious body of text. It's possible to feel these deeply rooted poems finding friends even as you read them. They will be spoken in resonant spaces to grateful congregations. They will find new homes in the middle of lonely nights. Generous renderings of familiar biblical stories and precious principles in her own inimitable voice. I bow down to 'An Uncluttered Gospel' and 'Navigating No' among so many gems and sing praises to Nikki for lifting us up."
     —**Naomi Shihab Nye**, Young People's Poet Laureate,
          Poetry Foundation

"'What is there / to recommend this world?' Nikki Grimes asks, a universal question any human being who has ever suffered has posed. 'One honest piercing look around /and there are tears enough /to wash away the world,' the poet acknowledges. The constant drum of sorrow, 'Drought famine / murder and mayhem / night terrors breaching / the brightness of day' all have the power to drive us to desolation. And yet, in the midst of her despair, the poet stops to listen and hears the answer to her prayer: 'God whispers in our ear / Look, to me! Look here!' Again and again in these poems, each of which serves as a powerful short homily and biblical exegesis, as well as poetic utterance, Grimes finds the grace she—and we—need to move forward and to do what Flannery O'Connor urges all people of God to do, to love the world even as we struggle to endure it. By turns celebratory and sorrowful, these hundred poems honor the movements of the restless human heart and offer a place of repose, bringing us finally to the joyful Good News that we need to be constantly reminded of: 'The secret's out: / the kingdom of God is here,' and we are in its midst."
     —**Angela Alaimo O'Donnell**, author of *Andalusian Hours:*
Poems from the Porch of Flannery O'Connor and *Love in the Time of*
Coronavirus: A Pandemic Pilgrimage

"These poems of Nikki Grimes are like sermons in the standard sense, but also in the original Roman sense of 'conversations'—clear, colloquial talk that is reverent about God and often gently irreverent about our failures to live lives of faith. The language of *Glory in the Margins: Sunday Poems* is clear and fresh, and the book's messages based on the Bible will be insightful and consoling for readers of all ages and backgrounds."
—**A. M. Juster**, poet, author of *Wonder and Wrath*

"Nikki Grimes is my big sister in the faith, and the poet laureate of Madison Street Church. Sunday in and Sunday out, with a raucous love for Jesus and a quiet intimacy with the English language, she humbly accepts the invitation, and takes the holy scalpel of God's Word to our small church community. She combines the truth and grace of scripture with a surgical use of Spirit-led words that cut away our pretensions, cauterize our fears, and call our souls to hope. Her poems, shared at the start of every sermon, constantly conspire to make me a better preacher, a better pastor, and a better person."
—**Rev. Jeff Wright**, pastor, Madison Street Church, Riverside, California

"Nikki Grimes has written many, many books of poetry during her esteemed career. But in this one, you hold more than just a book: you hold a sanctuary."
—**Sarah Arthur**, author, speaker, and editor of the Literary Guides to Prayer

Glory in the Margins
Sunday Poems

Nikki Grimes

IRON
PEN

PARACLETE PRESS
BREWSTER, MASSACHUSETTS

**For my Madison Street Church community,
Riverside, California**

2021 First Printing

Glory in the Margins: Sunday Poems

Copyright © 2021 by Nikki Grimes

ISBN 978-1-64060-677-7

Scripture quotations are from the New Revised Standard Version Bible, copyright © 1989 National Council of the Churches of Christ in the United States of America. Used by permission. All rights reserved worldwide.

The Iron Pen name and logo are trademarks of Paraclete Press.

Library of Congress Cataloging-in-Publication Data
Names: Grimes, Nikki, author.
Title: Glory in the margins : Sunday poems / Nikki Grimes.
Description: Brewster, Massachusetts : Iron Pen, [2021] | Summary: "A thirteen month cycle of poems distilled from chosen scriptures, viewed from her perspective as Black, as woman, as poet, and looking for the glory found in the margins of life"-- Provided by publisher.
Identifiers: LCCN 2021016483 (print) | LCCN 2021016484 (ebook) | ISBN 9781640606777 (hardcover) | ISBN 9781640606784 (epub) | ISBN 9781640606791 (pdf)
Subjects: BISAC: POETRY / American / African American & Black | POETRY / Women Authors | LCGFT: Poetry.
Classification: LCC PS3557.R489982 G57 2021 (print) | LCC PS3557.R489982 (ebook) | DDC 811/.54--dc23
LC record available at https://lccn.loc.gov/2021016483
LC ebook record available at https://lccn.loc.gov/2021016484

10 9 8 7 6 5 4 3 2 1

Published by Paraclete Press
Brewster, Massachusetts
www.paracletepress.com

Printed in the United States of America

CONTENTS

PREFACE

When was the last time you heard the words *poem* and *pulpit* in the same sentence? Likely as not, your answer would be never. Yet, if you've spent any time steeped in Scripture, you know that the Bible is rich in poetry, that poetry is one of its staples. You would never know that, though, judging from how rarely poetry makes its way into weekly worship services—unless you attend a small Brethren in Christ church in Riverside, California. The fellowship in question is Madison Street Church, and I am its Poet Laureate. For several years at Madison, I have had the opportunity to marry my poetry and my faith in worship. The poems in this collection were culled from those years, but Madison is not where my journey in creating poetry for worship began.

In 1978, I moved to Stockholm, Sweden, where I lived for six years. There, I became part of the international fellowship of Immanuel, a Swedish Covenant Church. Immanuel was easily the most diverse body I have ever belonged to, bringing together believers from as many as twenty different countries on any given Sunday. Even more unusual, however, was the way in which the leadership of our church embraced all forms of art in the worship services. Where most religious institutions employ music and decorative visual art, Immanuel threw open the doors to dance, drama, contemporary visual art, and poetry as well. If you had an artistic gift, room was made for it, and so it was Immanuel that first allowed me to bring poetry into Sunday worship.

My very first exploration of Scripture through poetry was the story of the Christ child told from the perspective of Mary. In a suite of poems that carried through the Advent season, I climbed into the skin of the young girl found in Luke's Gospel and felt the heart-stopping terror, awe, and finally, overwhelming peace of the Gabriel encounter. I contemplated the likely rejection of Joseph, her betrothed, imagined the stinging whispers of gossips who would, no doubt, question the timing of this pregnancy, and more. In so doing, I felt, in a visceral way, how monumental a thing it was for Mary to say yes to God in that moment, and to keep saying yes to him throughout the hard months and years that would follow. And as I brought my revelations to the congregation through poetry, their eyes were opened too. Listeners found themselves able to enter this sacred Scripture, this oh-so-familiar story, in a fresh, new way. And they liked it. As for me? I was hungry to do more.

As a person of faith with a reverence for the Holy Word of God, I also understand that God welcomes, and even invites, the honest questions of his children, and so I come to the Word with an open heart, bringing my questions with me. As I climb into the skins of the men and women I encounter in Scripture, I try to look at the world through their eyes, asking the hard questions of God that they must have asked, seeking the same solace, wisdom, inspiration, and guidance they must have sought. Of course, I am bringing my twenty-first-century experiences and sensibilities along for the ride, and so I also look for connections between ancient Scripture and the daily realities of my own lived experiences. That means, I'm sometimes referencing daily headlines and happenstances, alongside the words and experiences of

Abram and Sarai, Saul and David, Mary and Martha, Paul and Luke. And as I do so, I ask God to guide me, to shine light on those nuggets of truth he would have me share with his people. The Sabbath is his, after all. The pulpit is the place for his *Shekinah* glory, not mine. Bathing this work in prayer keeps me clear on that point.

Now, after years of doing this work, I've selected 100 of these poems to share with you. I've arranged them in a thirteen-month cycle, moving from January to January. Ninety-eight of the 100 were prompted by specific Scriptures, which are referenced at each poem's end. I love the way January is both an ending and a beginning, and so I chose to use poems from that month to bookend this collection.

Here you will find poems appropriate for high days on the Church Calendar such as Lent, Easter, Pentecost, Advent, Christmas, and Epiphany, as well as American holidays like Independence Day, Labor Day, and Thanksgiving. You'll even find an Earth Day poem within these pages, because no one has a greater responsibility to care for the earth than the people of God. No matter the topic, though, the focal point is always the Word of the Lord.

These poems were originally designed for the pulpit. However, they are also suitable for devotions, dramatic readings, and as part of choral performances. When strung together on a specific theme, they also work well for reader's theater presentations. But feel free to simply enjoy them as the poems they are.

JANUARY

His

The Father is unerringly faithful
to those who are his,
a belonging not secured
by shackles of iron that can be broken.
No. This belonging is sealed by
the blood and life surrendered
of a Son—his, a fierce bond
no sin or foul weather can untether.
Beyond blood brothers,
blood sisters, kin.
Our souls comingled for eternity.
We are his,
beloved children to whom he gives
grace abundant, healing, light,
the right to call him Daddy,
to crawl up on his knee
or rest against the chest
of the Divine.
Love is the only sense
we can make of it.
He is yours. He is mine.
All because he is faithful,
pouring out rivers of favor,
enriching speech, knowledge
and spiritual gifts,
doling out daily bread,
compassion, comfort, and strength
as needed, as promised until the end.
God has been, is, and will be
Faithful One, Sure Provider,
Fierce Protector, Holy Father,
Gentle Mother, Peerless Friend.
Peel back the layers of his huge heart
and find it ever beating for we
who are called his.

1 Corinthians 1:1–9

Purge

So often in the gathering gloom
Hope is the song we sing
both melody and lyric.
His name is Dayspring
whom we glorify.
Call him Hope personified.
And where would we be
without him?
Isaiah told it well:
the world was ever darkness
till he came.
The darkness threatens still
until he comes again.
In the meantime
in the in-between time
we follow the counsel of the one
crying out in the wilderness
"Prepare ye the way of the Lord."
We purge the closets
of our hearts
discard old resentments
unrelinquished
get rid of old hurts unforgiven
confess our own stubborn sin—
whatever it takes
to make room
for God's radiance to pour in
where it's needed.

Romans 15:4–13, Matthew 3:1–12

Drum Major

Cookie-cutter in hand,
we rush headlong
into the world
on a tear to make Christians
just like us.
But Father and Son corralled
a dizzying selection of servants,
implanting each
with a different word.
Young Samuel began with
the dark news of judgment
about to be delivered
against Eli.
Nathaniel was given
a brighter promise
of greater things to come.
Martin Luther King Jr. marched
as a drum major for justice.
All were assured
that the Good Lord
means business,
either way.
Whoever we are,
what matters is that
we hear him when he calls,
that, skeptic or not,
we respond to him
from the integrity
of our hearts,
that, joyful or jarring,
we handle his precious word
as something solemn, and alive.

1 Samuel 3:1–20, John 1:43–51

In the Silence

Timing is everything they say
and good things come
to those who wait.
Well waiting is hardly my forte
but a relay runner
practices patience
knows to study her teammate
monitor that runner's rhythm
in order to anticipate
the perfect passing of the baton.
One must wait in silence
watch for signs
like the First Begotten did.
Jesus knew who he would call
to run the race with him
had invested in their lives
learned the beating
of their hearts
and when at last he called them
his voice laced with love
was already familiar
his urgency easy to detect.
He knew the time was right
to step into the flow
of the Father's work
and so can we.
Study the rhythm of the Lord
practice his pacing
anticipate his perfect passing
of ministry's baton.
He will always let us know
when the time is right
if we wait for The Word in silence.
Lord, teach me to be quiet.
Teach me to tarry. For you.

Psalm 62:5–12, Mark 1:14–20

Singularity

Strident in our separate
points of view
we prove our preference
for tug of war over
the purposes of God.
Paul was not the last
to notice or give warning.
The heart is a single muscle
pumping life while it is whole.
Split or cracked in the middle
the beating stops.
Do we kill the God in us
so lightly?
Succumb to the division
of our ego and make
the singularity of God's purpose
a lie?
My way is best, we shout.
No! My way is best!
No! Christ is the Way,
the Truth, and the Life.
How quickly we forget.
Should the Savior
regret the crucifixion
his unspeakable suffering
to reconcile us to the Father?
He bartered his very breath
to make of us one body.
How goes that hymn, again?
We are one in the spirit.
Well, are we?
And if we are intent
on division, on war
who will be left
to feed the poor
to heal the sick
to spread the gospel
to build the kingdom
of Heaven?

1 Corinthians 1:10–18, Matthew 4:12–23

Gifted

We are the church,
a cathedral of grace,
built of living stones
each bearing a gilded gift
of the Spirit
offered for *El Elyon*'s glory.
Perhaps it's healing, wisdom,
or prophecy.
We might be tempted to say
My gift is better than your gift
but pride plays no part here
unless it's God's
since these holy talents
were plucked from the treasury
of his own Spirit.
The best we can do
is bear them humbly
and be ready to provide them
at the point of need.
In Cana, even Jesus waited
until the wedding party
ran out of drink before
transforming water into wine.
The truth is
he could have done that
at any time.
But *Yahweh* designs
a moment and place
for every gift of grace
he bestows.
Let us each receive our gift
whatever it may be
and look to the God of mystery
for further instruction.

1 Corinthians 12:1–11, John 2:1–11

Habitation

The Father has a penchant
for fixer uppers
we human houses with
peeling paint, rusted pipes
cracked shingles, faulty wiring
and shoddy foundations
desperately in need
of reconstruction.
No point in us
beating our chests
or patting ourselves on the back
after Christ is done renovating
our souls.
He's the one who gets credit
for making us beautiful.
Don't forget
we started off poor in spirit
meek and mourning,
parched and panting.
Before we could even imagine
inheriting the earth
we had to sink low enough
to comprehend the wisdom
of looking up.
Once we did
we found the Lord
waiting and ready
to make our fleshly houses
suitable for
his habitation
and his gift
of joy.

1 Corinthians 1:18–31, Matthew 5:1–12

Enmeshed

Come. Come and see.
—words that stir curiosity
and a twinge of fear.
After all, what will
befall us if we do?
An invitation to a party
tends to breed a bit of anxiety.
We hesitate to step into
a roomful of strangers.
Yet, John reminds us
we are known by
this particular host
who chooses to sanctify us
and identify us as Friend.
So we respond to
the Lamb's invitation
and dare to enter in.
No need for shyness in
the fellowship of the Son.
He created us for communion
for community,
bound us together
by love, grace, forgiveness
and once we are fully
enmeshed in his family
we are free to extend the invitation
free to say come
to those still standing
lost and lonely at the door
those wondering why
the peculiar man
with pierced palms
is smiling.

1 Corinthians 1:1–9, John 1:29–42

FEBRUARY

Fathomless

Peter has it all over us.
He heard the crackle of thunder
that spoke This is my Beloved Son
with whom I am well pleased.
And yet God made sure
that thunderous truth
cracked through the crevices
of our own beings.
The story is always the same.
We ball our puny fists
filled with the hot air
of our overblown egos
and strike out into the world
imagining we ourselves
will conquer all—
until we slam into the wall
of our shriveled limitations
and deeply sigh
or cry out to a healer
a miracle maker
we barely sense, or know
desperate for mystery
glory, redemption.
Wondrously,
the promised Morning Son
rises in our hearts
the heat of his glory
burning a tattoo on our souls
leaving the imprint of himself
God the Father—his father—
and the Holy Spirit besides.
And in this personal way
Immanuel is revealed,
this Jesus we barely know
even now. But how can we
possibly fathom
him whose pierced hands
hold the universe together

even while he deigns to dine
on the most meager of meals
with those of us hungry enough
to finally invite him in?

2 Peter 1:16–21

Indelible

As dark clouds gather,
we search for God's will
like hidden treasure
hunting for that all-important
X that marks the spot.
Yet, the Ancient of Days
is both mystery and open secret.
Forgetting that we whip out our
intellectual metal detectors and
hit the metaphorical beaches
listening for the beeps that tell us
where we should sink our shovels
to dig for Truth, or whatever promise it is
we *really* want.
We likewise go to Scripture
magnifying glass in hand
desperate for some special decoder
or that universal translator
we've seen on Star Trek
that can convert our tears
to language *El Shaddai* can hear.
But the one we serve is multilingual
and fairly plainspoken
even writing on walls
when necessary. Granted
we don't always embrace
his point of view.
Nevertheless, you must admit
the Father has a habit of posting
unobstructed signs
along the paths he has chosen
and painting
color-drenched pictures
across the clear or clouded sky
like those rainbow reminders
he set for himself, and for us
of the permanent covenant

between the Lord of Heaven
and man, and creature
a covenant of mercy
written in his own
indelible blood.

Genesis 9:8-17

Promises, Promises

I'm a stickler for
arriving on time
and keeping my word,
once given.
And yet, counting the promises
I have broken over the years
would break me.
Perhaps the same is true for you.
Good intentions notwithstanding
the happenstances of life
can intervene:
illnesses unexpected,
sudden storms that
clog our schedules,
even occasional lapses
in memory
can throw a monkey wrench
in the works of the word given.
But, as Abraham learned,
not so with God,
who called the Israelites
to bear the mark of covenant
in their own bodies.
Promises kept are God's
stock in trade.
A son of Abraham's
own aged flesh,
from his own withered wife
was one promise *impossible*
and yet God kept it
though Abraham,
tired of waiting,
tried to help God out
by having a child with Hagar.
Even then, God held to
his end of the bargain,
and laughter was born in Isaac.

El Olam's promises
grow more precious every day.
How strengthening it is to know
our Heavenly Father always keeps
his vows.

Genesis 17:1–16

A Time to Shine

I'm not sure
I ever rightly understood
the sacredness of Sabbath
a time of rest
spent with God, so vital
failure to do so
once held the penalty
of death.
The weight of worship
was—is—visible,
the *Shekinah* glory
a stamp of God Almighty
glistening on the faces
of those who dare
to draw near
the dearly beloved *we*
God's spirit-filled
living temple
those who most yearn
for transformation.
Like Moses we descend
the mountain of meeting
radiating from the kiss
of his glory—and not simply
for show-and-tell.
Adonai empowers us to be
like Christ
each a trustworthy servant
eager to soothe, encourage
help and heal
ready to wrestle evil
down to the ground
and to build up the body
standing on the
the firm foundation
God gave us
in the Lord.

Exodus 34:29–35:2, 2 Corinthians 3:12–4:2, Luke 9:28–43

The Bright Side of Repentance

Webster has got it wrong
this time.
Repentance is not
feeling regret
although we may.
Repentance is action.
It's that dirty little
six-letter word
we have all heard
and wish we hadn't:
Change.
Unfortunately necessary
it takes time, patience
and can even be
a little smelly.
We might need to
fertilize our roots
to promote new fruit.
Change is a tough taskmaster
demanding that we
break old habits
we would rather
bend and keep.
A white lie is not
really a lie. Right?
Wrong.
As distasteful and painful
as change may be
it is better than
the alternative:
Unless you repent
you will all perish.
That *you*
is we.
Ouch.

Luke 13:1–9, 1 Corinthians 10:1–13

One Cookie Leads to Another

Intense hunger
is a scream in the belly
piercing you from the inside out
demanding attention
the sorry state
forty days of fasting
will leave you in.
It is good to remember
that hunger carries no shame
but how we fill ourselves
may well be up for review.
If we knew
God was watching
how often would our hands
disappear inside those
cookie jars labeled
Do Not Touch?
It's a fair question.
I once turned myself
over to temptation
then swam in a bed of tears
from the guilt of it
suffered a string
of seemingly endless
sleepless nights
devastated that I had
so much as considered
ripping God's heart out
risking separation from my Lord.
No sin, however delicious
in the moment
is worth that.
So, the next time temptation
came for a visit
I rode that bad-boy out
basking in the smile of my Lord
as temptation's pain
slowly ebbed away.

Luke 4:1–13

Ribbon of Blood

What is there
to recommend this world?
Drought famine
murder and mayhem
the rape of innocents
night terrors breaching
the brightness of day?
One honest piercing look around
and there are tears enough
to wash away the world.
But God whispers in our ear
Look, here! Look to me!
And there we see
the ribbon of blood
that led to redemption
to restoration.

We count our blessings
and find forgiveness
provision peace healing
the sweet salve of
communion.

Our Father's beauty
is everywhere on display:
the velvet petals of a rose
the majestic wings
of eagle and hawk
as they split the sky.

We hear the treble of joy
rising from the congregation
and we tremble
with waves of praise.
Oh, God!
Good is your name
forever.

Psalm 111

Safe Deposit

Stress is a word
life teaches us to spell.
We are all well-acquainted
with worry
that wicked worm
that eats us
from the inside out.
Which goes to show
we are not as clever
as we imagine.
Bird-brained is hardly
a compliment,
yet our feathered friends
have the right idea.
They never sweat the details
like fretting about
where their next meal
is coming from.
They know *Jehovah-jireh*
is on the job.
The lilies know this too.
They leave their
fragrant finery
up to the Creator.
We would do well
to take note.
I remind myself
time and again
worry is a long jump
off a short pier.
It gets us nowhere
we want to be.
Better to invest
our spiritual currency in
the Bank of Heavenly Trust.
No deposit, no return.

1 Corinthians 4:1–5, Matthew 6:24–34

MARCH

Dancing on the Edge

Alone in the wilderness,
Jesus beat his body
into submission
with a fast, a cleanse creating
more inner space for spirit
to saturate the walls
of his being
bringing more holy focus
to his divine mind—
the purpose Lent
manifested to perfection.
Forty days alone
and famished from fasting
Jesus danced on the edge of delirium
and Satan thought the moment
a timely opportunity
for a duel with his enemy
imagining Jesus weak enough
to fold at any hell-born suggestion.
Turn these stones to bread, he said.
Throw yourself down
from this temple, he said.
Fall down and worship me,
he said. But Satan discounted
the mental dexterity
of our advocate's mind
the strength of his spirit
the sharpness of his holy sword.
It is written, said Jesus.
Man shall not live by bread alone
but by every word
from the mouth of God, he said.
Don't put the Lord to the test.
Worship the Lord your God
and serve only him.

Satan had failed to understand
before the duel ever began
the fix was in.
The Bread of Life had already won.
And because he did
so have we.

Matthew 4:1–11

Like Locusts

The season of lament
appears on no calendar
I can find
yet it can be counted on
to arrive on our doorsteps
uninvited.
We recognize the signs with
meteorological precision:
the gathering
of dark clouds
a smothering sadness
a swarm of
depressing thoughts
eating away at our joy
like locusts
and we withdraw
personal failures
our only companions.
Oh, yes!
The season of lament is here.
And where is our faith?
Why has it chosen
this moment to flee?
We hunt for that
trail of light
that speck of star-shine
that reminds us
God is neither dead
nor gone
nor done with us.
He has made promises:
I will never leave you
nor forsake you.
He will surely keep them
won't he?
Won't he?

Lamentations 1:1–22

The Sea of Despond

Lowered into the cave
of despair
I watch the darkness thicken.
The blanket of bleakness
smothers me until
I can scarcely breathe.
The cave walls echo
with the laughter
of my enemies.
Where is your precious Lord, now?
they taunt.
The question slams against
the walls of my mind.
Yes, Lord. Where are you?
Don't you see the perversion
of human rights?
Don't you care
about the hungry?
Daily injustices
leave layers of my heart
in bloody strips.
Free-falling into
an emotional abyss
I have yet to hit bottom.
For a brief moment
the notion of suicide seduces.
That's when the cave floor
rushes up to meet me
and my sin-broken soul shatters.
What is there left to do but cry out?
Jesus, have I lost your love forever?
The answer is whispered
in my ear:
"The steadfast love of the Lord
never ceases."

Ribs cracked
I breathe a little easier
clutching that glistening
hem of hope.
I finally settle into my grief
and wait for the compassion of
the Good Shepherd.

Lamentations 3

Jagged Journey

The still small voice
comes from within
part and parcel of
the new covenant,
the one that gives us
an intimacy
with the Host of Heaven.
If we answer the call
we are all in
ready and set to go
from darkness to light—
such a sweet invitation!
To serve, and to follow, yes!
But we are also wise
to take into account
the difficult corridors
the Lord's spirit-led footsteps
sometimes took him to
and through
amidst jagged rocks
past human snakes
and pausing painfully
in a place of thorns and skulls.
God makes no apology
for the circuitous route
to heaven.
But he promises
we will get there.
He will lead us and love us
on the journey
and our path will be marked
by his glory and the good
he means to make of us
in us, and through us
along the way.

Jeremiah 31:31–34, John 12:20–33

Marching Orders

Christ has a penchant
for sending us on odd errands.
Ask the early disciples
dispatched to a stranger's home
in order to borrow a colt
this in a culture
with zero tolerance
for thieves.
A risky business
at the very least
especially for followers
who didn't comprehend
the why of it all.
The Lord had a purpose
of course.
He always does.
But how often are we
let in on the secret?
Every day, the Lord
calls us to tasks
that seem to have
no rhyme or reason
errands that appear to be
questionable, at best.
Go into the world
and love your enemies.
Put the needs of others
before your own.
Bless those who
despitefully use you.
Forgive the unforgiveable.
Give yourself away.
Strange errands, indeed.
And what do we say?
Is there a yes
on the tips of our tongues?

Just as at Bethpage and Bethany
the Prophet understands
the why of his call
and in the end
that's all we really need
to know.

Mark 11:1–11

Inauguration

How often do we
take the Holy One of Israel
for granted
assume he will work
according to
our ill-informed dictates?
Assumptions are easy
but they're frequently
a mistake.
Remember the Triumphal Entry
the expectation that King Jesus
would wipe out Rome
with a mighty wave of power
and inaugurate a newer
kinder, earthly kingdom?
Of course Messiah
had something else in mind
and the crowd's Hosannas
boisterous as they were
and smattered with blessings
merely paved the way
for disappointment.
Wailing waited
in the wings.
Assuming had blinded them
to the truth of the moment:
The triumphal entry
did not mark
the beginning of the end
for Rome
but the end of the beginning
of God's Kingdom
one not of this world, at all
but of the heart.
So, come,
Son of The Highest
you of infinite surprises.

Take your seat
on the throne
of our lives.

Mark 11:1–11

46

Worth

Judas loved the feel of cold coins
rubbing together
in the palm of his hand
but Mary preferred
the fragrance of pure perfume
lavished on the feet
of her Heavenly Master—
something special
for someone sacred.
Still, it was less
than he was worth.
Carve the name of this radiant one
upon your heart, he
who paints the world with light
and writes his love for us
in blood.
Who is this Root of David
who strikes the rock
and raises water
in the wilderness
causes rivers to run
in the desert?
And what does
he require of us?
Honor and devotion
obedience and praise
as lavish as Mary's
expensive perfume.
It's a matter of priority.
We owe him skin and bone
heart and breath
for deleting eternal death
from our stories.
Our talents, our tithes
our bodies
as living sacrifices—
is anything too much
to surrender?

Ask Judas
whose cold coins
failed to satisfy
his soul.

John 12:1–8, Isaiah 43:16–21

Aftermath

Angels in the daytime
are anything but routine.
Yet there they were
reciting the impossible
like old news:
He is risen.
My mind still stuck
on that stone, wondering
who rolled it away.
Were the disciples
stuck on that, too?
Or was it the missing body
or the eerie way
his clothes were left behind?
Sometimes we tend
to miss the point.
He. Is. Risen.
Now comes the work
of building his kingdom
of reflecting his light
through the transformed lives
his bloody sacrifice
made possible.
His end, a new beginning.
His death and resurrection
an arrow pointing us
in a new direction.
Lord, may we, like arrows
bend ourselves
to your touch.
May we fly straight and free
wherever you
would send us.

Luke 24:1–12, 1 Corinthians 15:19–26

APRIL

The Sad Parade

Sorrow clung
to every footfall
of the women
wending their way
to a tomb
that marked an ending
they could scarcely bear.
We feel the press of death
weighing down
their shoulders
even though we know
the true end of the story
is only the beginning:
the Beloved rising
strong and clear-eyed
his mortal wounds
only evidence of his love.
Go and tell, he says
his voice still ringing
in our ears.
He is *here*
the very poetry of God
beautiful in passion
in holiness
his full-to-bursting heart
ready to lead us—
flawed and puny as we are—
in the mighty work
of building his kingdom.
Do not be afraid, he tells us.
And why should we be?
He's already taken
the worst that could happen
and turned it
into victory.

Matthew 28:1–10

Mourning Obscurity

Ravaged by the jagged claws of loss
I understand Mary's heart,
a fissure of flesh
erupting with sadness,
her sight compromised
by the mysterious mist
of grief.
She is hardly
in a state of mind
for rhetorical questions.
Knee-deep in heartache
she leans into a tomb
meant for the dead
and is asked by
strangers in white
why she is weeping
as if tombs and tears
don't naturally go together!
And then, from another
an inquiry even more inane:
Who are you looking for?
A loaded question
don't you think?
But her mourning obscures
what history and we
see as obvious:
You are looking for the living
among the dead.
Only her beloved's voice
can cut through the chaos:
Mary! says the one she seeks.
Lord! And her search is ended.
But who are *we* looking for?
The babe in the manger,
the itinerant teacher,
the preacher,
the healer, the friend?

Or the Lamb sacrificed
the Christ
risen from the dead to be
our all in all
forever?

John 20:1–18

Zero Balance

I see my new home
rooms framed by Your
pure white bones
walls shimmering red—
the mansion You build for me
in the hallow of your heart.
Crimson is the color of love
the new sacrifice
followed by
your resurrection
the red sea you invite me
to swim in.
Better than grain
or silver or gold.
The old sacrifices were
a temporary good
but the Ageless One
had something more
eternal in mind
the kind of sacrifice only
his own Lamb without spot
could provide—
a permanent ransom of souls
meant for transformation.
Why love one another
even when it's hard, even
when it hurts?
Why forgive?
Why live for others
who may not even notice?
Think blood-stained thorns;
Think blood-smeared sword;
Think blood-soaked nails.
Think cost. Paid. In. Full.

1 Peter 1:17–23

Alpha and Omega

Uncertainty seems
the watchword of the day.
Fear is folded into
too many moments.
Images of terror
crowd our newsfeeds.
Sound health and employment
slip through our fingers
and, time and again
our *terra firma* shows itself to be
anything but.
And yet, in the midst of all
if I surrender to stillness
your voice
slices through the darkness.
Come! Come to me, you sing,
grace ringing in your words.
You who was and is
and is to come, reach out,
and I think about
the horrors you withstood
to purchase my peace.
The Thomas in me
is finally silenced.
I lose myself
in unmixed praise.
I close my eyes.
My face against the cool tile
of your throne-room floor is hot.
I peek, lids trembling
and spy
your strong bronze feet
the holes still there.
You Alpha and Omega
touch me
though I do not
burn away or wither

which causes me to marvel
at the way you
wield your power
and your love.

Revelation 1:4–8, John 20:19–31

Earth Day

Eden tells us
the great I AM
is partial to gardens
to displaying his love
in the face of a flower.
The Creator of giants
he himself
treads the earth tenderly.
Why not we?
Why not choose
bipedal motion or bicycle
over the standard vehicle
belching poison
into the air?
Why should we care
you wonder?
Our Heavenly Father
asks us to follow
in his footsteps.
He has always known
how to love the earth
how to tuck his creatures
in for the night
how to fill their bellies.
He has modeled
what it means
to watch over raven,
magpie, sparrow. Man.
God himself
has shown us how.
Now all that remains
is that each
in his or her own way
say, Yes, Lord.

Job 38:41, Luke 12:6

Bitter Pill

Underneath the sleek mask
of cool and nonchalance
we are all tender-hearted
victims of the unforgiveable
each with a
somebody-done-
me-wrong song.
We drag around ropes of anger
we are always in danger
of tripping over
or hanging from.
Forgive, the Bible tells us
and we think, Sure!
That's easy for you to say!
But hey
the Omnipotent One
knows exactly
how impossibly painful
forgiveness is
which is why he offers
to do the hard part for us.
Joshua shows him
rolling away
the disgrace of Egypt
as only the Almighty could
just as he would roll away
any unspeakable crime
done against us.
No sin is too heavy
for the father to roll away.
The prodigal son's brother
forgot that
and who could blame him?

He had earned the right
to his anger
and wasn't ready for
the power of forgiveness
to take it all away.
Are we?

Joshua 5:9–12, Luke 15:1–32

Personal Epistle

Dear Self,
remember: virtue lives
on the other side of redemption
through the door of the Word
in all its fullness.

Enter in to discover strength
to withstand every temptation
to find refreshment
at each battle's end—
and yes, there are many.

Know, use, and rely upon
holy Scripture to learn
discernment, and to wisely divine
the secret strategies
of the enemy.

Even in our weakness
he is no match for those
who cling to
the One True Logos.
Still, our adversary is wily.

He will twist the Father's Word
if we're not careful
if we don't have the truth
tattooed on our hearts
like our Wonderful Counselor.

The enemy can only
pick God's Word apart
if we don't know it, if we don't
own the Word-Walking
for ourselves.

Matthew 4:1–11

Macedonia

In Macedonia
on the Sabbath
Paul and Silas
looked for worshipers
outside the gate.
Isn't that often
the kind of place
that draws God's attention?
There they found Lydia
and other women
gathered by a river
the very site where
a woman washes clothes
and God washes hearts
as he did this particular baptism
blessing Lydia and her family
to come to him, fully.
But what if the vision that led
Paul and Silas to Macedonia
had been of a *woman* calling?
Would they have been
equally earnest in coming?
God knows.
It's just a question.
And who was Paul looking for?
And what did he expect
to find or to do?
Isn't it true
that so much Kingdom work
happens when we're on the way
to where we imagine
the Lord wants us?
It doesn't really matter I suppose
so long as our hearts
are as open as Lydia's,
ready and waiting for
whatever vision,
or commission
the Father chooses to send.

Acts 16:9–15

MAY

Prickly Promise

Fresh wounds and invisible dog tags
mark us as soldiers of the cross.
Yet we haven't always understood
the war we signed up for.
Suffering is a word we would rather
forget how to spell.
Lord, you know this well.
We love you and like Peter
we swear to sacrifice our lives
except that death and dying hurts
even when it is
the crushing death
of dreams.
It seems you offer us life eternal
and internally, we calculate
a journey heavenward
without despair or pain
or persecution.
Still. Darkness fights
to extinguish our Light,
the prickly promise of thorns
is everywhere
and the wilderness
is a given.
Why else would you promise
to make a way through it?
A paradigm shift is needed, Lord.
Help us beat the Enemy
into full retreat.
Help our hearts embrace—
not the suffering,
but you in the midst of it.
Help us celebrate
the opportunity to see
your grace and glory
revealed.

1 Peter 4:12–16, 5:6–11

Bare Hands

Secrets in the night
shared openly between
holy man and Holiest
the latter, the giver of life
the former, a religious leader
longing for the nearness
of the man of miracles
thirsty for the taste of a spirit
he could not name
and so Nicodemus came
bearing a bowl of need
too full by far already
with inherited half-truths
peppered with
human understanding:
Can one enter the second time
into the mother's womb
and be born?
The wrong question, indeed.
Little wonder
the gift of spirit offered
is so rarely received.
We must come instead
with only the cup
of our own bare hands
then hold them out, empty
and leave it to the Lord
to do the filling.
He has spirit enough
to pour out
for us all.

John 3:1–17

Holy Discomfort

God means to rattle our bones.
Lest we miss it
a violent wind is prelude to
the Holy Spirit's dramatic arrival—
no brimstone, but tongues of fire.
(Where do you think Kilauea
got its awful power?)
Yes, the Lord intends
to shake things up.
On Pentecost
Adonai put out the call to all
who might dare to love him
degree of melanin
never part of the equation.
To make it plain
he spelled out his invitation
in a myriad of languages.
Say what you will
about nationalism
white or otherwise
El Shaddai's prismatic kingdom
beats it every time.
Black or white, slave or free,
Jesus died and rose again
for you. For me.
The Gospel could not be clearer.
This new day heralds prophecies
and dreams of the divine
generously showered among
man and womankind.
And what?
What are we to do with this?
Shout. It. Out!
In this world divided
the secret of unity is ours!

Jesus Christ and him crucified
the body and blood
we partake of
in common.

Acts 2:1–21

70

Daily Planner

I tag each day with purpose
type in a list of to-dos
on the digital calendar
of each 24-hour cycle.
Oh, I'll leave a moment or two for
the unexpected, but only grudgingly.
I want to be able to look back on
a day of checked boxes—
the illusion of control.
I find it laughable in a way.
Call yourself a Christian
and mean it
and Jesus will be
all up in your business
turning your enemies into friends
telling you who your brother is or is not
calling you to walk on water—please!
Read Acts if you think I lie.
As much as I protest
the best parts of the day
are the surprises, the interruptions
that shatter all my best intentions.
When they're good, they are very good.
But when they're bad, they are even better
because they chase me to the altar
to cry out to the great High Priest
who dismantles my plans
in order to produce patience
reconfigures my schedule
to remind me of the sacred
and teaches me that growing pains
most often apply to faith.
Preach all you want
Jesus says
but until the Holy Spirit
breathes into a moment
your words and works
are merely hollow.

Study to show yourself *approved*
not glued to the spot
you have settled on
apart from me.
Set aside your
carefully constructed programs
and preconceived notions
of who I am or who I love
and simply follow Me.

Acts 10:44–48

Entryway

Imagine a place
where darkness and sin
are less than memory.
All light. No night.
Glory walking
up one holy boulevard
and down the next.
No sun, moon,
or lamp required.
It is a place of
dreams come true
chiseled from
love's cornerstone
by the architect of wonder
each facade
glistening like gold
at high noon.
Open gates
flaunt the freedom
of the New Jerusalem.
Forget passwords
and secret codes.
Those written in
the Book of Life
those brimming with light
simply walk right in
the Lamb's name beaming
from their foreheads—
the one tattoo
I am eager to receive.
Forever rolls out
like a carpet
and the Beloved are invited
to step lively.
This is a world
worth waiting for.

Revelation 21:10, 22:5

Pentecost

Heliga Gud,
vi prisa dig
in every language
with every breath
that you give us
just as you breathed into
Peter and the others
gathered on that
Pentecost morning.
Herre Gud
the Spirit parts our lips
for every Hosanna
from Alaska
to the Horn of Africa,
from Australia
to the Swiss Alps
from Juno
to Jerusalem
we celebrate your majesty.
Tongues of fire
the beginning of power
of signs and wonders
being parceled out among
the children of the king.
We cry Abba, Father together
the Spirit binding us
across time and territory.
Jesu Kristi
we call on thee
for renewed power
to finish the work you started
of loving the broken
back into the arms
of the Lord.

Acts 2:1–21, Romans 8:14–17

His Hope

How sorely do we grieve
the Holy Spirit
when we shrivel
our true value,
crawl into some dark cave
carved of the enemy's lies.
Enough!
He who walks in glory
calls us friend!
King of the Ages he is
and elder brother too
always on the lookout
for our highest,
his final will and testament
for each of us
written in blood:
That we should know
one another
in the deep communion
he shared
with the Father
hearts set
to the same clock;
that we should walk beneath
the great and infinite guard
of God's holy wing;
that—sweetest of all—
we, the called
whom he entrusted
with the treasure of his word
should altogether inherit
his joy!

John 17:6–19

A Good Bet

An old story, a bold story
of Elijah, as showman
of Mount Carmel
setting a grand stage on which
Jehovah would tell
the tale of his power.
All smoke, no mirrors, full flame.
Theatrical, yes.
But hardly a game.
Call down fire from
the god you serve,
said Elijah
to the followers of Baal.
Then I will do the same.
The deity who sets fire to the altar
and swallows the sacrifice in flame
is the One True God.
Time to go all in
thought Elijah.
Time to set the record straight.
To stack the deck
Elijah ordered
his wood and sacrifice to be
doused in water till the altar
all but floated away.
No man can ignite wet wood.
Of course, it was no man
the prophet called on.
Label his risk calculated.
His faith, daring and confident,
invites us
to be and do likewise
because the Deliverer is true
and, as Paul reminds us
his gospel is the one
we can count on.

1 Kings 18:20–39, Galatians 1:1–12

JUNE

Vessel

Clear as crystal
ritual is
an empty vessel
the weight, color
beauty or ugliness of it
depends on
what sits inside.
It cannot hide
the dark pulp
of a poisoned heart
the muddiness
of murderous intent
or envy
green as gall.
Gossip Avarice Adultery—
all sin shows through.
All holiness too
and generosity
and love.
Yes, ritual has
its own beauty
like cut glass reflecting
bright rainbow shards
wherever the light lands.
Yet the vessel is neither
light nor rainbow
and no ritual is
of itself
holy.
But we can be
if we fill ourselves
with the Lord.

Mark 7:14–23

What Slinks Away

Often with the arrogance
of distance
we consider the disciples
trembling in that locked room
and we shake our heads.
But the spirit of fear
that gripped them
is all too familiar.
It's not of God, we know
and yet we entertain it
worrying what people will say
keeping ourselves sealed away
in the safety of our
comfort zones.
We hide from possible ridicule
or persecution
until in walks Jesus
passing through our defenses
ghostlike
and bearing Peace
derision and death
hardly a match for him.
Receive the Holy Spirit
he says, and suddenly
fear pads out the door
tail between its legs.
Clear-eyed now
we stare into the Lord's face
and await instruction.
Leave this place, says Jesus.
Go out, my Word in hand
and spread it far and wide
to the world of
women and men
for whom I died
for whom I live
again.

John 20:19–23

Legacy

Legacy
a word that brings
a sparkle to the eye.
In Abraham's day
it was all about the heir
the one through whom
one's name would live on.
Addicted as we are
to the Now
the story of Abraham and his progeny
teaches us the value
of the long view.
The sometimes shadowy road
Abraham and his people
passed through
was marked by heartache
betrayal, famine, alienation
and for a bleak tunnel of time
slavery and oppression.
This the dim road
that separated Jehovah's
precious promises to Abraham
from fulfillment:
A late-in-life son
through Sarah
descendants numerous
as the stars
a land of milk and honey
set apart for his people
and a permanent place
in the pantheon of prophets—
a legacy he was able to attain
to achieve, to receive
because Jehovah was along
for his journey
as Jesus is for every step
of ours.

Genesis 15:1–20

God's Kitchen

It seems a simple choice:
faith over law
but faith leads to freedom
and freedom frightens.
Our flesh would rather cling to
the seeming safety of walls
and to-do lists with neat boxes
we can check off or crawl into.
We do so love painting ourselves
into corners or escaping
into the mountains
imagining Jezebel
on our heels
especially when we feel
naked and alone.
But then comes faith
ushering us into
a world of the miraculous
as when God fed Elijah
from his own kitchen
sent angels to his side
bearing jars of refreshment
to quench his thirst for water
and companionship—
though in truth
he was never really alone.
There were 7,000 souls
as faithful as he.
Yes it is faith that leads
to community.
We drape ourselves in Christ
the patterns of our lives
blend with his
and we become one:
rich and poor, slave and free,
man and woman, you and me—
beloved all
and welcomed equally.

1 Kings 19:1–18, Galatians 3:23–29

A Page from the Pharisees

Solomon was right.
There is nothing new
under the sun.
Man is an old hand
at corrupting God's word
at using psalm and proverb
as excuses for evil in disguise.
Rather not honor
a needy parent with
the fruit of your labor?
Just give more
to the poor, right?
Wrong. Half a truth
is still a lie
but we try it anyway,
figure out some
double-speak
that lets us say
we are honoring
the commandments
when we're not.
Jesus reminds us
that God sees all.
Much as we might like,
we cannot pull the wool
over his eyes.
With one voice
we swear Never!
and tell ourselves
how thoroughly
we despise the Pharisees.
But we had better be wise
to check the mirror first
to look deeply
find whatever small way
we do the same
then pray:
Father, forgive us.

Mark 7:1–13

Amendment

Good soil sounds like
a once-for-all proposition.
If you have good soil
you're golden, right?
But when was truth
ever that simple?
Do we not amend the soil
in our garden each spring
to make it better?
Do we not fold in
bone meal and compost
to enrich our rose beds?
Some questions
are worth asking.
Do we not all suffer
rocky seasons in life
during which the Word is
difficult to digest
or even to receive?
Is that not when endurance
is required?
I am simply asking.
Can good soil become barren
if left unchecked?
Mustn't the soil itself
be nourished
after wind and storm
have swept the good we see
on the surface
clear away?
Believe that all in life is static
if you choose
but even good soil needs to be
turned and tilled
nurtured now and then.
Come Lord! Bring us fresh seed

after removing
whatever is acidic
in our souls
so that our soil becomes
fertile ground for your Word
once again.

Luke 8:5–14

The Meaning of Manna

Imagine: Rush hour
on the way to a local mount.
Jesus knew a thing or two about
the stress of daily life.
The desperate crowds
clinging to the hem of his robe
made it plain:
wants pressing in
on every side
misery multiplied
by loneliness, poverty,
food all but forgotten
in the hunger for healing.
How often are we
crushed by need?
Yet, Christ gave us
the secret to survive
and to thrive:
we must slow long enough
to feed on the Holy.
Oh, the body has use for
baskets of bread and fish
but what about
the manna of God's word?
We must pause to bathe
in the soothing waters
of his spirit
leave the weight of worry
behind
so that we can meet
the requirements
of the next moment
and the next
and the next—
Refreshed.
Refined.
Renewed.

Mark 6:30–56

Number One

You, Heavenly Father
are at the top
of my daily docket
right there
in my devotions.
Try not to dig into that
too deeply.
I am not in the mood
for confession.
But my impression from
commandment #1 is this:
when I entertain other gods—
and who does not—
I had better place and keep them
behind the line You've drawn
in the proverbial sand of time.
I am yours and You are mine.
I—we—shall have no gods
before thee:
not money, not sport,
not celebrity,
not anything or anyone
before You
your Holy Spirit
your chosen Son.
Adonai, El Berith,
El Shaddai,
You, alone
are Number One.

                    One—a number so small,
                    yet encompassing all.

Once we're clear on the Who
we are free to focus on the What
that matters to you.
We are listening Lord.

Our Kingdom calendars
are ready and waiting
for your heart to fill them in.
Almighty God
worthy of our devotion
what is your instruction?

Exodus 20:3

JULY

Petition

We are all adept
at the loose use of language
flinging words about
like so much confetti.
But intercession
is no casual endeavor, no sweet
I pray the Lord my soul to keep.
Intercession is deep soul-work.
To intercede is to plead with God
on behalf of another
slipping on another's skin
standing beneath the canopy
of another's sin
and asking the
inventor of mercy
to forgive us both.
Daniel modeled the truth for us:
We are all guilty of something
as recently as yesterday,
every one of us, going back to Moses
to Abraham and Sarah
to Adam and Eve.
God sees us for who we are.
To go before him
we must first agree.
Then it is on us to recall
the very nature of this Holy Father,
his splendor, his might,
his glorious grace
proven through the ages.
Only then are we prepared
to pray for another
groaning with as much passion
as we would summon for ourselves.
Dear Abba, please hear our petition
we who are desperate and unworthy
we who are called
by your name.

Daniel 9:1–19

Daily Dependence

The Holy Book is laced
with lessons in prayer
some delicate as spider-silk
some rough as a sailor's knot.
And then there is Hannah
who prays with specific intent
for a son, Hannah who prays
with full abandon from
the deepest recesses of her heart
propriety and restraint forgotten
her river of words unrehearsed.
No neat formulaic request
flows from this breast
only the agony of a heart
about to break from the strain
of desires unmet.
Which begs the question:
how do *we* pray?
Perhaps we should
spend some time
pondering the particulars.
For now, we know prayer
is a two-way conversation
and from the other side
before Hannah's answer is provided
comes the healing balm of faith
the substance of things hoped for
the evidence of things not seen
the quiet assurance
that prayer has been heard
God's Word delivered in silence—
his gift of peace
an answer in itself
a lesson in prayer
worth noting.

1 Samuel 1:20

Transparency

Transparency
is not our go-to in this world.
Most of us
would rather masquerade,
pretend to be strong, confident
completely put-together
more often than not.
On a good day
one might even
consider oneself
a great catch for God
someone who can
make him look good
by association.
Laugh if you want
but who practices humility
unless the moment is clutch
unless life lays us flat on our
inabilities to meet
our own needs?
Jehoshaphat knew how to
come to El Shaddai
hat in hand
prostrate in his demeanor
as he stood in the temple court
with all of Judah in audience.
Fast! Pray! he pronounced
his kingly dignity tossed aside.
We need you, Adonai—true ruler
of the nations, he cried,
his desperation
on full display.
That's the way to do it
acknowledging our powerlessness
and God's holy might—
our brokenness an open book
laid before the one
who saves us.

2 Chronicles 20:1–12

Hoarder Control

Imagining ourselves enlightened
the thought of Aaron's
Golden Calf
tends to make us laugh
but where is our
moral high ground?
Blocks and blocks
of storage lockers
line our roadways
the new cathedrals at which
we worship the coarseness
of too many possessions.
Are these not the bigger barns
the rich man in Luke conjured,
the shallow places created
to house the hollowness
of things?
Oh, Jehovah-jireh is pleased
to feed the sparrow
dress the lilies of the field
and provide
everything we need
but after all our grasping
leads us past praising God
for the good gift of himself,
the time comes to clear the shelf
lay everything
on the altar, once again
seek first the kingdom of God
cry out, Father, forgive us!
then, prostrate before him
and ask Lord, what would you
have us do
with these gifts?

Luke 12:13–21

Doctor in the House

He slogged through
the world of sound
without hearing even
his own footfalls
his brokenness
on parade
whenever he opened
his mouth to utter
a muffled stutter.
Thank God for friends
who took pity
and led him to the Lord
the fount of blessing
we all need
to stand under.
When the Lord
performs his wonders
and we are healed of
whatever ails us
sin or sickness
how can we not
run through the streets
crying out his name
singing the praises
of the One
who made us whole?
And if we fail
are we perhaps
blind and deaf
to the miracle
ourselves?

Mark 7:31–37

Seven Baskets

Stomachs growl
and reason is forgotten.
All we can manage to focus on
is the deep bowl of our need.
Jesus knows, and fills us.
He has had plenty of practice.
Once—no fairy tale—he turned
a few fish and seven loaves
into seven baskets, plus
enough to feed four thousand.
Then came the Pharisees
chasing signs. But where were they
when the thousands feasted
on the miraculous?
This is nothing new: people whose eyes
are tightly closed to the truth
scream at the top of their lungs
"Show me! Prove who you are! I dare you!"
And what do they get for their trouble?
The Lord pulls up anchor
and sails in search of listening ears.
Well, he is here. Now.
Are we listening?

Mark 8:1–13

It's Mathematical

The Tent of Meeting
was a shared responsibility.
The call for holy heavy lifting
went out, all Levites represented.
Yet young and old
were left without assignment
the why—a mystery to me.
In any case, life equals change
and today's church
casts a wider net.
Our Tent of Meeting
offers something
for almost everyone to do.
Yet needs announced
are regularly sifted like flour
and too few bend to catch
what remains.
Do the shy wait
for personal invitation?
Let it be known: more yeses
are frequently required.
On the other hand
some prideful parishioners
who stand to be counted
insist on the ridiculous sport
of solo-serving
staggering under weight
never intended for
a single pair of shoulders.
We occasionally forget
the we of God
his membership in a Trinity
his divine workload shared
by the holy Three-in-One.
The mathematics of
The Book of Numbers
suggest we humans adopt

a broader mantra:
Here we are, Lord.
Send us.

Numbers 4:20–49

Brothers John

Electricity is such a mystery.
Throw a switch
and your room is ablaze.
Throw it again
and you are doused
in darkness.
Light comes, light goes.
A hero knows
what matters is the light
you carry in you
and out into the world.
John Lewis is
a shadow chaser gone home.
He reminds me of another
one affectionately nicknamed
The Beloved.
Slip into the skin of a child
for a moment. Sit cross-legged
round John's campfire
singing hymns as he regales us
with tales of
the Son of Righteousness
who walked the earth
the one whose aurora lingers still.
Close your eyes
then open them again
in the spirit's realm
as dear John asks
Who's your Daddy?
And, what do you want to be
when you grow up?
If you are blessed to belong
to the Lord of Glory
you will answer
without hesitation
God is my father, and
I want to do, commit to

and be like Jesus
the Holy One of God.

1 John 2:28–3:10

AUGUST

Reel vs. Real

At first glance,
the human imagination
seems boundless.
Wonder Woman and Thor
charge across our vision
Mozart, Salvador Dali
and Shakespeare
make us gasp.
DaVinci taught
the Wright Brothers
to dream of flight
we have since superseded.
But in truth

                    our imagination
                    is stunted.

We could never
conjure a God
whose waves buoy us
whose words refresh us
whose spirit satisfies
our deepest thirst.

He is our rock, yet
we swim in his mercy.

He redeems us from the river
of doubt and death.

He drowns us in love
and drenches us in hope
drawn from the well
of his own being.

All this in the midst
of life's pain and affliction.

However much
the darkness encroaches
keep your imaginary heroes.
They've got nothing
on our God.

Psalm 42

Bend. Bow. Now.

Here, poem meets prayer.
We are exceedingly comfortable
with posturing and self-defense
that masquerade as apology.
But what is needed
in this moment
is unmixed confession
of our nation's sin,
deep and indefensible.
Now I lay me down to sleep
must make way for
something more muscular:
sackcloth and ashes,
prayer and fasting,
naked prostration
before the Lord.
Daniel understood
radical repentance
begins with this
unvarnished profession:
You are righteous, Lord
and we are not.
Father, please heal our nation.
Cleanse our stubborn hearts.
Show each of us
what part to play.
Broken as Judah and Jerusalem
we cry and come
bending our will
toward the good
God dreams for us still
no matter our sin
no matter what skin
we're in.

Daniel 9:1–19

Fueling Station

Ready or not
here I come!
a gleeful warning
chanted in childhood
often followed by giggles
or delightful
peals of laughter.
Be ready for
the Lord's return,
Luke tells us
his tone an exhortation
of the serious kind:
Be attentive to the Word
and enthusiastic about
its execution.
Our action plan is this:
Pray without ceasing.
Feed the hungry.
Visit the sick.
Remember the prisoners.
Pursue justice.
Above all, heed the call
to be generous
with the grace given.
Much is implied.
Some days, the challenge
weighs heavy, yet our
kingdom-inheritance assured
we are free to
give ourselves away
amassing heavenly treasures
as we do.
As for keeping our lamps lit,
the Morning Star
has provided
all the fuel
we'll ever need.

Luke 12:32–40

Team Jesus

Unity: more precious than we know.
We love to flex our Christian muscles
recite Scripture blindfolded
while standing on one leg;
roll out reams of hermeneutics
laced with Hebrew vocabulary
dusted with a bit of Greek;
sing hymns till the rafters shake.
But what about our
Oneness in the Spirit?
Paul heralded the importance
of safeguarding the love between us.
Unity in Christ is our strength
which makes it a sore point for Satan.
What better way to try to break
the back of the church
in an age of division
then by sowing dissent?
His mandate is clear:
Weaken the foundation
of the unity God breathed.
Let's name the original
dissenter-in-chief
drive him to his home
on the shores of Hell!
The work the Lord has called us to
he has called *us* to—together.
Male and female apostle alike
sacred, secular, deacon, dispatcher,
church mother, mayor,
Bible teacher, truck driver,
preacher, poet—
all who, broken, bloodied and reborn
are blessed to serve
in the house that Christ built.

We are Team Jesus
rallied round a call
requiring God's strength
but also the unity in Christ
he has instilled
so that we, *together*
can Do. His. Will.

Romans 16

Hurricane Paul

Paul blew into Ephesus
on the winds of the Holy Spirit

hovering there three years
raining down extraordinary miracles

through the Word and the words
of the gospel, till all of Asia

was soaked with mercy—
a holy hurricane with Jesus as the eye.

Then came the long, trembling goodbye
woven with warnings of savage wolves to follow

hungry for newborn souls. But there were
assurances, too, of God's gift of strength

and grace towards the sanctified.
The apostle's passionate mission ended

in a flood of tears with one last good word from
the Master: It is more blessed to give than to receive.

Then Hurricane Paul blew out to the sea
that would carry him all the way to Jerusalem.

Acts 19:1–12, Acts 20:17–38

Peculiar Commission

Paul might have called his story Poetic Justice
once persecutor, now persecuted for his faith:
stoned, beaten, and drowned. Yet the alternative
was darker by far: No God. No light. No life eternal.
I read of brothers and sisters in China, in India
tortured and raped for the crime of believing
and I, from my relatively safe perch in America
hesitate to even utter the word persecution.
Even so, we too are among God's peculiar people
commissioned to die daily, to sacrifice secure
socially acceptable lives in favor of the sacred
the God-breathed life of inspiration, of faith
at any cost including trouble. But cheer up.
This life is a short trip, my friends, and
our final destination is golden.

2 Timothy 3:10–17

A Garden of Stories

The book we live by
is filled with poetry
but precious few pleasantries.
It's best to expect
a chronicle of challenges
proverbs pregnant with warning
promises of trouble in this world
prophecies of division
in place of peace
testaments of bloodshed
and lamentable lessons
we would rather not learn.
This, mixed with free-will
is the soil we were planted in.
And any gardener can tell you
seeds seem to have a mind
of their own.
Place them beneath
a bowl of sun
shower them with
nature's champagne
nurture them with plant food
and still there is zero guarantee
they'll produce the fruit
you intended.
Good grapes or wild?
I guess it all depends
on whether we lean into
or away from
the Son.

Isaiah 5:1–7, Luke 12:49–56

Mad Street

What was it that drew me here?
The slow heartbreak of disappointment
sent me in search of a new holy home,
a new gathering place of the broken
a movement less from than to this house

of unrehearsed warm embrace
of coffee and conversation shared with
the fluid ease of family ready and waiting
to welcome this odd, irreverent puzzle piece
nobody even knew was missing.

There was something about the quietly messy
madness of holy construction that never
pretended perfection, a place of constant
reinvention, ever revising this particular
fellowship story, so long as God was always

to be found living between the lines.
There was something about a place where
hard questions of God were dared out loud,
and often, and I don't know could be
the acceptable answer. Something about a place

where liminal became a space for me
to hang my hat. Even the name was a
certain kind of crazy, and crazy works for me.
We are all a little bit mad, now aren't we,
this gang of peculiar people who dare to

believe in God and act like it? So,
whether present in body or not,
at any given time, this Mad Street
is the intersection of home, and holy,
for me.

SEPTEMBER

The Joy of Jubilee

How shortsighted that we
created for communion
too often choose
the monument of labor
to prostrate ourselves before
pouring out our hallelujahs
to the 24/7 god of industry
Jehovah-Shalom reminds us
of Jubilee
that even the earth requires rest.
We frail humans function best
by honoring the Sabbath.
We frantically punch
the proverbial clock
forgetting that renewal
and regeneration
are the precious rewards
for sanctifying the seventh day
and keeping it for the Lord
for the blessed baptism
of his holy presence.
And so, Father,
as Israel was taught
we set aside our labor today
and come before your throne
to celebrate your creation
and the myriad of ways
you've delivered us
this week, alone.
To keep our hearts
from becoming stone
we lift them, now
silent and still
waiting to be filled anew—
with You.

Deuteronomy 5:12–15

Sticky Fingers

Even those of us who grew up
grubbing pennies know that we
in the industrialized West are drunk
with plenty, fat with an overabundance
of everything we're told we deserve.
How easily we buy the lie! Never mind that
all our stuff leaves us wanting, our hearts
rumbling loud as our bellies, our souls
wondering where contentment went.

How difficult for us to fathom the joy
of, say, the poor in Calcutta slums, or
indigenous families huddled in hovels
in undeveloped corners of the world.
But what lights many of them from the inside
is their own generosity with one another.
Note, the poor are always faster to offer
a crust of bread than the rich are to invite you
to a meal of extravagant gourmet delights.

The poor, though, have wisely perceived
Life's secret. Open-handedness, while costly,
is always compensated with boundless
treasure: a tickle in the soul, a gladness,
a moment of pure joy— the natural reward
for sharing. We who have much
foolishly cling to our coins with
sticky fingers, learning late that there is
little joy in the dark of a miserly heart.

Acts 20:32–35

Keeping Accounts

The morning news anchor delivers
the latest atrocity like a dump truck
releasing refuse at our front doors.

Injustices run rampant today. As a child,
I'd hear the old ones say God don't like ugly,
a precursor to assurances that God will

right the wrongs. But how can God keep up
when ugliness multiplies like cancer, its dark cells
on a mad march across the belly of the earth?

The Word promises me that God will call
the unrighteous to answer for their sins. But
how can God keep track of the multitude

slithering out from under the rocks where
they lay hiding? The percentage of evil
might lead one to worry whether more than

a few will get away, unless you remember
the God of Numbers, the Holy Accountant
mastering digits from the start: two by two,

two shall become one, 70 x 7, double-winged
creatures, four-gated cities, twelve disciples,
and God, himself—a member of the Three-in-One.

Who better than he to keep records of both
the righteous and the wicked? Not one particle
of wretchedness is hidden. Not one bit of ugliness

or beauty, or devotion, or servant sacrifice
gets by him. The God of Numbers knows best
how, and when, to balance the books.

Numbers

Stuck in Bethesda

How smug we are, sifting through our
carefully sourced and meticulously sorted
files of financial institutions, fashion outlets

produce markets and urgent care facilities—
forever certain we know precisely
where to go to acquire whatever we need.

Our vision is so focused on
our pools of Bethesda
we sometimes miss the

wounded hands held out to us
by the Lord. What if the paralytic
trapped in his broken body

for thirty-eight years, balked
at Jesus asking, Do you want
to be made well? and chose

to cling stubbornly to the way
of healing that he knew
when Jesus ordered him to

stand, pick up his mat, and walk?
Likely, he'd have stayed a paralytic.
How often do we remain sick, or

otherwise suffer need because our
minds and hearts are closed to God's
inexplicable manner of miracle?

Time to set human wisdom in
its place, look up from our own
pools of Bethesda, lift our eyes to

the one with healing in his wings.
We've all heard the saying:
It's not what you know, but who.

John 5:1–8

The Mark of Cain

See the heart of God
embossed upon his word
bits of it rolled out in
the fine strips we call
the Ten Commandments.
Thou shalt not kill
is more than celebration of
the sanctity of life.
It's designed to protect both
possible victim and
would-be perpetrator.
Think, here, of the soul
how murder leaves a stain.
Remember the Mark of Cain
the burden of his sin
the living death
his murder of Abel left
in its wake?
Deny this if you choose
but the capacity to kill
resides in the very tips
of our fingers.
Rage visits us all, my friends.
Cain raised his hands in anger
and lowered them in shame.
The Lord would spare us
the prison of that sin.
God's highest hope for us
is freedom.

Exodus 20:13

Storm Watch

A world in distress
shouts gloom and doom
through a megaphone
until our ears bleed.

Floods come, unbidden
storms rage, without apology
or warning, the earth shakes
and splits reminding us that

terra is not so *firma* after all.
And yet in the midst of it
as we scurry to tape window
panes to protect them from

shattering, or hastily pack
suitcases to outrun firestorms
raging nearby as we stumble
heartbroken beneath the

agonizing weight of grief or
grow battle-weary in a world
of uproar, backbiting, and war—
in the midst of all the Lord whispers,

Fear not, and God calls to us
from the center of himself and says
Come, child. Snuggle with me for
a while. Rest, here in the silence of

my love. The time of my eternal reign
is near, but for now, return to me
often. Remember: my perfect peace
is always here waiting for you.

Psalm 46

What Can I Get for You?

Work done for and benefit conferred
upon another is how Webster defines
service. You'll notice, there is nothing

demeaning in this definition.
We humans have added that
all on our own. Anyway, I cannot lie:

images of nights out on the town,
waiters and waitresses working
at my behest, seem pretty sweet.

My selfish heart leans in for a listen.
To be the one conferred upon has
a nice ring to it—until a truer word

creeps in from the mind of Christ
I've said yes to; Christ whose
thoughts were once and always

streams forever flowing towards
the needs and benefits of others;
Christ who served us the bread

of his body, filled our goblets with the
wine of his blood. He lived and died in
praise of servanthood.
Should we do less?

Philippians 2:5–8

An Uncluttered Gospel

The shared burden
of the everyday
may sound like a fairy tale
but the early disciples
lived that story.
Houses, furnishings
and goods in common
they chased God
instead of things
finding time left over
to meet the needs of those
around them.
Wrestling on their knees
in corporate prayer
little wonder
their community
routinely experienced
the miraculous—
though no miracle
is ever truly routine.
What are we missing,
we relatively affluent?
Can any of our goods
ever equal God's?
Maybe it's time to
review our possessions
remind ourselves
who owns them
spend more time together
in prayer
and spread around
whatever wealth
we have on loan.

Acts 2:42–47

OCTOBER

Who Can Spell Despair?

The heartbeat of need pulsates in the street.
We hear it from the safety of our windows:

the poor, the sick, the disenfranchised,
the neighbor who is lonely. They might

cry out for help if only they knew who to call.
The Lord waits in the wings, invisible to

the naked eye, but you and I can see him.
He holds the bowl of answers, of blessing

in his pierced hands. Shall we tell them?
Shall we shout it out? Come! Taste and see

that the Lord is good! The despairing among us
are desperate for reminders.

Psalm 34:1–8

Remedy

Too Late—two words
that lay heavy
in the tight confines
of human language
squeezed next to
the word impossible.
But the Christ will not be
so constrained.
Ask Lazarus. Ask Mark.
Remember the woman
healed of a hemorrhage
a disease no doctor
could remedy?
All she did
to secure her healing
was touch the hem
of Christ's cloak.
Then there was
the dying child
the Resurrection
was delayed in reaching
before she expired.
Yet, one should never
confuse delay
with denial.
In ordained time
Messiah made quick work
of the young girl's
perfect healing.
"*Talitha cum*," the word
he spoke, and speaks, to spark
every soul inclined to listen—
the dead of heart, mind, spirit.
Rise up! he said
and the child rose.
It was just another healing
and resurrection on the sly.
All power. No limits.
One Lord.

Mark 5:21–43

Aslan

He is not like us.
We fear forgetfulness
run from the devastation
that it can be
while he chooses
selective memory
a grace he bestows on us
to remember our sins no more.

He is not like us.
We prattle on about
promises, promises
proclaiming our cynicism
with every know-it-all sneer.
But the Redeemer's
unbreakable promises
are sealed in blood
wrapped with wonder
and tied with bows of blessings
to be unfurled
each day tomorrow brings.

He is not like us.
We cling to the familiarity
of past failures
while he flings our
broken vows away
offering instead
a fresh covenant:
His love and faithfulness
his law tattooed on
the tablet of our hearts
his presence as palpable
as our pulse.

True to the word in Jeremiah
he makes us his habitation.
Praise him who is in us, now!
But remember:
He is not like us.
Amen? Amen.

Jeremiah 31:27–34

Fulfillment

In this whatever generation
contracts have all but lost
their meaning.
They are flimsy things
to lose, to shred, to flippantly
ignore, or break.
We love the loophole
and hate the fine print unless
it serves us.
My meticulously composed
contracts are rarely read
before they're signed.
The giveaway is always
the blank stare or, Huh? What?
whenever I raise some salient point
clearly stated therein.
But that response won't work
in the courts of heaven.
God is old school. His contract
cannot be lost, or shredded.
Ignore or break the particulars
at your own risk.
Don't lie. Don't steal. Don't neglect
to keep all the commandments
or else.
Sign this agreement? Yes!
Nevertheless, one warning:
it's useless to look for loopholes.
And, lest we forget
God's contract is a living organism
unlike any we've ever seen.
It's amended by Grace—*Grace*,
complete with a new bill of rights
for the redeemed,
giving the forgiven a free pass
into the Holy of Holies
granting us direct access to
the King of Kings.

And the old law?
Perfectly satisfied
by the only one qualified
to sign the dotted line.

Exodus 20:1–17

Navigating No

I am intimate with rejection.
As an author,
it goes with the territory.
On any given day, a No
may come in over the transom.
You learn to shrug off
the disappointment
and move on.
What choice is there?
Rejection is a door
with only one handle.
Ask Jesus.
He went back to Nazareth once,
his limitless power brought low
by the hollowness of faith
he found there.
Despite all they'd seen and heard
too many hometown hearts
shriveled by constant unbelief
proved unfit chalices
for the miracles
he stood ready to pour.
They say the Lord was
amazed, astonished, astounded.
Even so, he shrugged it off
peered into the future repudiation
his followers would face.
Move on, he said
preparing them.
Preparing us.
Shake the dust off your feet.
Then go. Stir every ember
of faith you find.
Blow on it with his Word
until it flames.

Mark 6:1–13

The Plot Thickens

The Mount of Olives,
the site of a small commission
and a necessary obedience:
two disciples dispatched
to acquire a colt in
shall we say
a questionable manner.
And soon thereafter
all is set for a demonstration
of power and humility
intertwined.
Enter our carpenter-king
who calls the dead to life
who silences the roiling sea
who gives vision to the blind
yet does not seem to mind
riding atop a borrowed ass.
A living, breathing paradox
he willingly approaches
the scene of the crime to be.
Come! Die with me,
he invites us
and drunk on the power
we have witnessed
we follow.
But what do we do
with the love that
held the Lord of Lords to the cross
in blood and agony
he could easily
have wiped away
simply by stepping down
and leaving us to pay
for our *own* sins?
How can we begin
to respond to that?

We bow our heads
our hearts, our knees.

Luke 19:28–40, Philippians 2:5–11

Irreplaceable

I'm single, by choice, an old maid
in yesteryear's vernacular, a spinster.
So what would I know about fidelity?
Well, maybe to an idea,
or a dream I've wrestled with,
clung to in good times and bad,
for better or worse.
But that is not marriage
so I guess I really don't know
about faithfulness—unless
it's to a friend, whose secrets
I hide in my heart
whose blessings I cherish like my own
whose heavy head I welcome
whenever my shoulder is required.
Then there's my country, 'tis of thee
which I am free to reprimand
because I'm family, and only want
what's best.
Still, that is not exactly the same as
fidelity to my one and only beloved
who I come home to, rain or shine
to share intimacies and
whatever kind of day I've had
then fall into his arms for the hug
I trust him to know I need
which, come to think of it
is an awful lot like my relationship
with the Lord, complete with vows
made, broken, and renewed after
the umpteenth time I have asked for
and received forgiveness.
God's Faithfulness
and his forever love
is what our bond is based on—
that irreplaceable thing
that gives me wings.

Exodus 20:14

Camel's Hair

Peek-a-boo is
the innocent art of surprise.
All it requires
is a pair of hands
covering a face, then
whipping those hands away
in one swift movement.
Of course,
the Father's surprises are more
the masquerade variety.
He turns up in places
we'd never imagine
raises the dead
speaks through an ass
uses anglers to fish for men
and repeatedly chooses
the weak over the strong.
Surprise!
He sends messengers to alert us
but they are nobody's
popular picks.
A few occasional priests?
Who can tell, considering
some behind masks
of unimpressive vagrants
like the one poorly attired
in camel's hair
surviving on locusts and honey
and living where? The wilderness?
Hardly the neighborhood
of choice!
A new baptism and
an unexpected Baptizer
is on the way, says he.
And guess what?
This surprise is only
the beginning.

Well, come, Lord Jesus.
Your people are desperate for
the sacred surprise
of your glory, however
it may appear.

Mark 1:1–8

NOVEMBER

Rose of Sharon

We speak of Sonrise,
the amber glow that kisses
the horizon of the world
with limitless luminosity.
A mighty candle is he—
No. A flame, fueled by
love and compassion,
a fire that burns away
the darkness of our heart
if we let it.
If we let *him*.
If we do the bidding
of the Spirit:
visit the sick, feed the hungry
pray that the blind may see.
Work the works of him
who sent me, he tells us.
That's the secret to
keeping his gift aflame.
Tend the Word
stoke its truth, every ember.
Spread the luminescence
until each corner of the city
shines with the afterglow
of grace.
Each place we're planted in
is meant to be
a boulevard of lights
scattering the choking smoke
of night
painting a bright path
to the Rose of Sharon
visible for miles.

John 9:1–7

Jezebel

Truth or Dare is not a game
the Church should play.
Faithful or faithless, holy or hellion
pure or defiled, take your pick.

You might say Thyatira
tried to have it both ways.
Loving and committed servants
on the one hand, and on the other

passively permitting one sinful pied piper
to lead the faithful away. Jezebel had to go.
Time and distance make that seem so obvious.
But is there ever a Jezebel in our own house

in our own heart, a part of us
pulling away from the Lord?
When we wrestle with right and wrong
is it Jezebel whispering in our ear?

Stand strong, says the Bible.
Do the Righteous Father's work
until the end. The Morning Star waits
to greet each who conquers
with a crown.

Revelation 2:18–29

Return Engagement

The evening news chronicles
the woes of the world.
We feel the press of darkness
leaning in, evil dancing
its final fury.
Who can deny it?
Yet, even at
the bleakest moments
the aurora borealis
reminds us
radiance and beauty
are always near.

Beyond the Christmas crèche
look to the sky.
Notice the clouds destined
to cushion those precious
pierced feet
as the full-grown
Son of Man
appears on Earth, again
his legion of angels
in tow.

Beware! Be awake!
we are cautioned.
Watch!
Be like children
alert to the sound
of reindeer hooves
on the rooftops.
What promised gift
can begin to match
the coming of his presence
his return
for us?

Mark 13:24–37

Love American Style

Love is a word tossed
flat as a Frisbee
while we trade in
rom-coms, soap operas
and dance-worthy pop songs
either saccharine or lusty.
But what does true love look like?
It is verb, not noun:
It is the stranger fed
housed and clothed
Good Samaritan-style
no drumroll please
nothing fancy, simply
good old-fashioned caring
for a neighbor, defined as
another, anyone hungry
or in need of a hug
no translation required.
Love is never caged, fenced
or barbwired
neither is America First
a slogan
you'll ever find
in a kingdom
soaked in the crimson
of a sacrificial love
that sent a savior
to the cross.
Love pulls its boots on
steps out into
the muck of the world
hands outstretched
asking, as God calls us to
What can I do to help?

Mark 12:30–31, Matthew 22:36–40

Out of the Frying Pan

Exile is a word
we assign to the ancients
or to people
other than ourselves.
But there are horrific
moments in this life
that force evacuation
from our places of comfort
times when storm clouds gather
pain beats us like a drum
the dreams we cling to
go up in smoke
and dystopian fantasies
seem all too real.
But even as wildfires
real or metaphoric
drive us into the wilderness
our good God whispers:
Go. Build, design,
sculpt, dance.
Write, paint, plant,
marry, and multiply.
Use the gifts I your God
have given you.
Care for the earth
and pray for the city
I send you to
and know this:
the God who shaped you
with his own hands
yet has good plans
for you.

Jeremiah 29:4–7, 11

Epilogue

Daily, we pray down justice
for a world in short supply—
and we are wise to do so.
The trouble is, we imagine
a clean thing, something
pure and bloodless.
Yet refined gold
and the searing fire that shapes it
is what should come to mind.
The prologue to peace and justice
is a dark story, a plot
marked with fear, boding
and distress upon the earth.
Our promised hero arrives
with angels wielding swords.
Quick! Turn the page
and you will find
the powers of heaven shaken.
The closer we get
to justice and redemption
the more we should
expect to feel
the quake beneath our feet.
The preceding chapters
of this story
warned us of death
and mayhem.
Fortunately
we've been invited
to read ahead
to see the Hope that lives
between the lines
where the Lord is
arms outstretched
waiting to guide us safely
to the end of the story
where peace and justice
reign supreme.

Jeremiah 33:14–16, Luke 21:25–36

Pitcher of Plenty

Mark and the other insiders
kept a careful catalog
of the Lord's provision.
Four thousand fed here
five thousand fed there.
Even so, they eventually
lost count.
You might as well
try to tally
the grains of sand
that edge the sea
as track the Lord's
miraculous provision.
After all
Jehovah-jireh is
his middle name.
Yet, the minute need
rings our doorbell and
we stare down at
our empty hands
rather than look
to the God-man
who holds
the pitcher of plenty
ready to pour it out
should any believer ask.
Blind as we can be
I wonder when we
will finally understand
that little is much
in God's hand.

Mark 8:14–26

Advent

We mourn the destruction
of Jerusalem,
wince as slim hopes
are bruised
beneath the heel
of the enemy.
Our hearts seem
too heavy to sing
but the song
is not forgotten.
We must cling
to the lyrics
if only in silence,
live in the rhythm
of the songwriter,
praise him and find reason
to dance again
even on the streets
of Babylon.
It is right to weep
at the sight of
evil unfurling
but only for a day.
Our cities are
awash in anguish,
desperation darkens
every door
every window
and now more than ever
we bearers of
his incandescence
must shine.
We will not dance
for the evil master
nor entertain
the tormentors
but we must sing out

about the Lord
who has already written
the last lines of our lament.
He is our Advent.

Psalm 137:1–6

DECEMBER

Solomon's Sentiment

Six years in Sweden taught me
the challenge of Winter Solstice.
Twenty grinding hours
of darkness per day
can slay the soul unless
you fill them with meaning.
I learned to celebrate the winter
with a blaze of candlelight
evenings of knitting by the fire
and the dizzying aroma
of fresh bread
turning golden in my oven.
I would marvel at each young girl
parading through the *Jul* market
balancing a crown of
fake candles on her head
reenacting the part of Santa Lucia
bringing light back into the world.
I close my eyes and remember
snow sparkling in moonlight
slow sips of spiced wine
tickling my tongue
and warming my insides
the soft crunch of just-baked
ginger cookies
munched after a night of caroling—
each a seasonal thing
marking a certain time of year.
We humans are geared
to respond to seasons
different dates on the calendar
different passages of our lives.
We resonate with
Solomon's sentiment:
For everything there is a season
a time for every matter
under heaven.

There is one matter, though,
linking all our days:
In every season
our God is worthy
of our praise.

Ecclesiastes 3:1–8

Favored One

I'm a sucker for
those tales of origin
where the hero or heroine
comes to life on
the wrong side of the tracks.
The storyteller speeds us back
to the site of shack, or hovel
or humble village
like, say, Nazareth.
Here, the Heaven Express
makes a single stop
and out steps The Messenger
wings neatly folded away
brightness his only uniform.
Our heroine is immediately
distracted by his greeting
and why wouldn't she be?
Seriously, who in his right mind
would call anyone living in
a penny-ante town like Nazareth
blessed or favored?
And yet Gabriel
called her favored twice
lest anyone forget.
Oh, the Gabriel–Mary encounter
is certainly well known
but it's the details
we need pay attention to.
What made Mary favored
in the first place?
Was it perhaps that she was ready
to bear the impossible
to carry the Christ inside her
no matter the cost?
And are we ready to do the same?

If so, by God's grace
we each wear this soul's tattoo:
Favored one.
And we get to carry
the Christmas gift
of the Lord's Light
wherever there is sunrise.

Luke 1:26–38

Skin

Some heroes of the day
make a brief appearance
in the story of God but
keep that old saying in mind:
there are no small parts, only small actors.
So the curtain rises and
in staggers Joseph, seriously sober
but suddenly knocked sideways by news
that the belly of his betrothed
swells with the son of another.
Heart shredded, our gallant hero's
first concern is the dignity of the one
he believes has betrayed him.
He swallows his pride
and decides to wrap her secret
in a cloak of silence
to protect her from disgrace.
God is of course the author
of this particular love story
so there is a supernatural twist:
an angel visits Joseph in the night
outlining God's plan for Joseph to marry
Mary, his faithful servant, after all.
And the remainder of the tale
centers on Joseph's surrender:
surrender to a life
of certain complication;
surrender to joining Mary
on a journey of mystery
and the likely threat
of whispers by gossips;
surrender to forfeit his rights
to the marriage bed until Mary
gave birth to someone else's son.
God knew this was
a lot to ask of a man, which is why
Joseph's willingness was required.

Ours too whenever God calls on us.
Surrendering our will for his
is how we show our Heavenly Father
that we choose
to have skin in the game.

Matthew 1:18–25

A Proper Introduction

Here he comes,
the Word walking
in a pool
of his own light
Son brighter than
the orb he created
to sizzle its way across
the daytime sky.
He is more excellent
than the angels
bearing the imprint of God.
This near-twin likeness
to the Almighty
is beyond extraordinary.
And if anyone asks
this Heir to the throne
this Son of Goodness and Grace
was no afterthought.
His spirit lived, spoke, was
from before the beginning.
But we humans
only came to know him
as the Babe.
As we smile down
on the manger
tempted to coo
and tenderly tickle his toes
it would be wise to recognize
the shadow of the cross
darkening his swaddling clothes
and what it cost
the Only Begotten
to pave the way
for our reconciliation
with God.

Hebrews 1:1–12, John 1:1–14

The Dance

Spiritual wallflowers,
we once were accustomed
to hanging back
frustrated and forlorn
belonging to no one
we could see
until he came
the same who brightened
Simeon's eyes
and Anna's.
He drew us out
onto the dance floor
our feet resting atop his,
children that we were.
He smiled
introduced us
to the Father
and called us family
before we could
truly fathom the miracle
of redemption
of adoption.
Now we waltz into newness
caught up in the music
whether the chords
are sweet
or discordant.
We need only
follow the steps
of our perfect partner
lean into
the Redeemer
and dance
delighted, at last
to be chosen.

Galatians 4:4–7, Luke 2:33–40

Sky Watch

You'd better watch out!
How does that song go?
He knows when you
are sleeping.
He knows when
you're awake.
He knows if you've been
bad or good, so . . .
you know the rest.
Sounds like Santa has
ripped a page from the Word
doesn't it?
But Old St. Nick
is talking about
presents in the present
not the gift of life eternal.
Santa, no matter how jolly
is not the reason for joy
or why we need to be alert.
Nor do we wait
for the Lord's
first appearance.
It's his second coming
we look forward to
the dream
of ultimate deliverance
light shattering darkness
once and for all.
It's the promise of God's
forever presence
we dare not miss.
It's the "not yet—but almost"
we hold dear.
The when of it all escapes us.
So, what is the point of living like
Christ is, once again
about to appear
like he's almost here?

The attentive waiting
gently goads us to good works
helps us to strive to be holy—
right now.

Mark 13:24–37

Living Proof

Zephaniah tells us a day will come
when rejoicing will pound the air like a drum

when the D will be plucked from disaster
when oppression and injustice are crushed

under the heel of the Holy One, when our Redeemer
will restore all that the locusts have eaten.

But what will get us there? Not the slogans we so
cleverly conceive: What you see is what you get.

Let go and let God. Walk the talk. It isn't talk that matters.
No amount of hermeneutical eloquence or hip and holy

millennial rap will feed the hungry, give respite to
the refugee, or comfort the distressed. In a contest

with intellectual belief, daily practice wins every time.
Living out God's word is the bridge between now

and the day of rejoicing before the throne.
Offering water to the thirsty is the key.

Do we believe in the Christ of Christmas?
You know what they say: the proof is in the pudding.

Zephaniah 3:14–20, Luke 3:7–18

Magnified

I love how stealthy
the Lord is.
Heralded by a few insiders
like Micah
the great I AM
came on tiptoe
hidden behind a mask
of human skin
sliding into the world
through a slip-of-a-girl
named Mary.
Breathless in her expectation,
she and her cousin Elizabeth
magnified the Holy One
who arrived at a locale
least expected
through a family hailing from
a humble city
of no particular repute.
Security for his people
sewn into the pocket
of his heart
Peace is
the great gift he brings
a strange trade
for sins confessed.
Yes, this Lord of ours
is a mystery.
Castles and senate chambers
are not
where you'll find him.
He lives in the souls he has
harvested for Heaven
a kingdom where love rules—
not the politics of power.
Look around.

The Beloved is here
hidden as always
in plain sight
waiting to be magnified
by us.

Micah 5:2–5, Luke 1:39–55

JANUARY

Full Circle

Here we go again,
January, its own Genesis:
a new ledger we line
with daily to-dos
intentionally determining
the content
of our tomorrows.
But we are not alone in this.
Before night and day
were Christened
God chose, planned
destined, and purposed
the scope and weight
of our moments.
He marked our calendars
with trial and blessing
his holy heart the image
bleeding off
the opening page
with glory in the margins
redemption and grace stitching
the months and years together.
Our Father left little
to chance.
And yet he risked it all
by granting us
the radical costly gift
of Will—
to choose what he
has chosen for us
to seek and savor his counsel
about the details
of our days
to always wrap our lives
in the lavish love
he offers
laced with new beginnings

and delicately designed
to see us through
the winters
of the world.

Ephesians 1:3–14, Genesis 1:1–5

Just Wait

Equity is elusive
this side of the veil.
Poor Lazarus
now resting in
the bosom of Abraham
could certainly tell the tale.
But justice in full measure
churns in the heart
of the Lord
building towards the day
it will be poured out
on those who need it.
In the meantime
in the lean time
when evil swaggers through
our towns, villages, and cities
masquerading as victorious
now when the blood
of our brothers and sisters
cries out from the earth
we cling to the Mighty Judge
and all-knowing King
who needs no
man-made video
to search out
the truth of the matter.
He scans the whole world
and every heart in it
with the piercing power
of his limitless light.
And at the appointed hour
Justice will rain down
and our parched souls
will thirst for it
no more.

Luke 16:9–31, 1 Timothy 6:6–19

Beyond Immersion

Intellectual assent
is only the beginning
of faith's story.
Next comes the call
for baptism.
But water, even blessed
is only wet.
Water alone
could not account for
the way John spoke
truth to power
or how he could hear
the thoughts of those
who imagined
him to be Messiah
then tell them plainly
he was not.
Something stronger
was at work in him
a power beyond immersion
that only descends when
we bow our hearts
before the Father
and confess our need
to be blessed
to soak in his Spirit
to drown in his love.
And so, like Jesus,
we wade in the water
and wait for the dove
hands outstretched
ready, at last
to receive the plenty
God has had for us
since Eden.

Acts 8:14–17, Luke 3:15:22

Message from the Father

The secret's out:
the kingdom of God is here
with all authority given
to rebuke evil
restore good
promote peace.
Yes! The time is here
for spiritual triage
for family members
ailing from the cancer
of depression
for marriages bleeding
on the side of the road.
The enemy is intent
on gnawing our joy
like a bone.
We must become
that Good Samaritan.
Sweet greetings and holy kisses
are not enough.
We must perform the stuff
of mercy, of deep prayer.
We must come alongside
offer the shelter
of our love.
Oh, Holy Father
move us from
our complacency.
Let us not be spectators
of hurt and misery.
Breathe on us a spirit of unity.
Convict us so that
we come to be
your healing hands
right now.

ACKNOWLEDGMENTS

Every book published has a team working behind the scenes. For *Glory in the Margins*, that team included Sarah Arthur, who believed enough in this project to direct me to Paraclete Press editor Jon Sweeney. Thanks, Sarah, for your excitement about the possibilities of this collection.

Thanks to my wonderful new editor, Jon, who embraced my vision for this book, and then broadened it with ideas that were subtle, and yet exactly right. Every author should be so lucky.

Thanks, as always, to Amy Malskeit, the best beta-reader on the planet. You have encouraged me at every leg of this journey, and carried me along on the wings of prayer.

Special thanks to Brethren-in-Christ Pastor Jeff Wright who, years ago, said yes when I asked if I could create poems to accompany his Sunday sermons. What a gift it has been for me to tithe my talent through worship services!

Thanks also to the members of Madison Street Church who have received this offering, week after week, year after year, and always asked for more. If you hadn't, this book might never have come to be.

Thanks to the Academy of American Poets for originally publishing "Bend. Bow. Now." under the title "You Still Dream," in Poem-a-Day on August 7, 2020.

Thanks, lastly, to anyone who has ever heard me read one of my Sabbath poems and asked, Could I get a copy of that? Finally, thanks to *Glory in the Margins*, I'm able to answer Yes!

IRON
PEN

"O that my words were written down!

O that they were inscribed in a book!

O that with an iron pen and with lead

they were engraved on a rock forever!"

—*Job 19:23–24*

Outcast and utterly alone, Job pours out his anguish to his Maker. From the depths of his pain, he reveals a trust in God's goodness that is stronger than his despair, giving humanity some of the most beautiful and poetic verses of all time. Paraclete's Iron Pen imprint is inspired by this spirit of unvarnished honesty and tenacious hope.

OTHER IRON PEN BOOKS

Almost Entirely, Jennifer Wallace

Astonishments, Anna Kamieńska

The Consequence of Moonlight, Sofia Starnes

Cornered by the Dark, Harold J. Recinos

Eye of the Beholder, Luci Shaw

Idiot Psalms, Scott Cairns

Still Pilgrim, Angela Alaimo O'Donnell

To Shatter Glass, Sister Sharon Hunter, CJ

Wing Over Wing, Julie Cadwallader Staub

ABOUT PARACLETE PRESS

PARACLETE PRESS is the publishing arm of the Cape Cod Benedictine community, the Community of Jesus. Presenting a full expression of Christian belief and practice, we reflect the ecumenical charism of the Community and its dedication to sacred music, the fine arts, and the written word.

Learn more about us at our website:
www.paracletepress.com
or phone us toll-free at 1.800.451.5006

SCAN
TO
READ
MORE